ZARIA'S GARDEN

Saturd
with Daddy

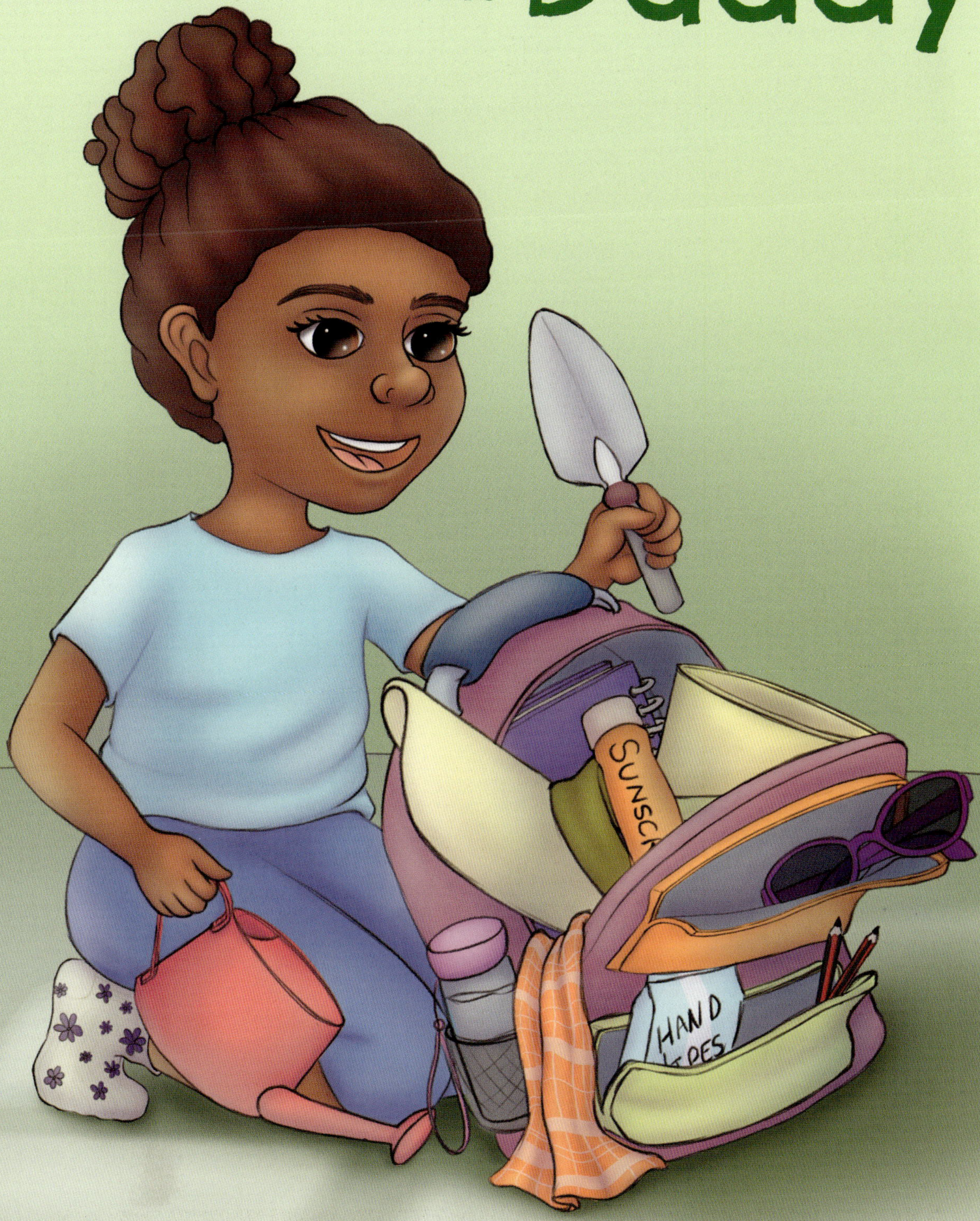

Thank you, Daddy, for teaching me how to farm. —ZJ

To my little one, you are my heart, my joy, and my inspiration. I am thankful and forever grateful for every moment I get to share with you. *Matthew 5:16* —KJ

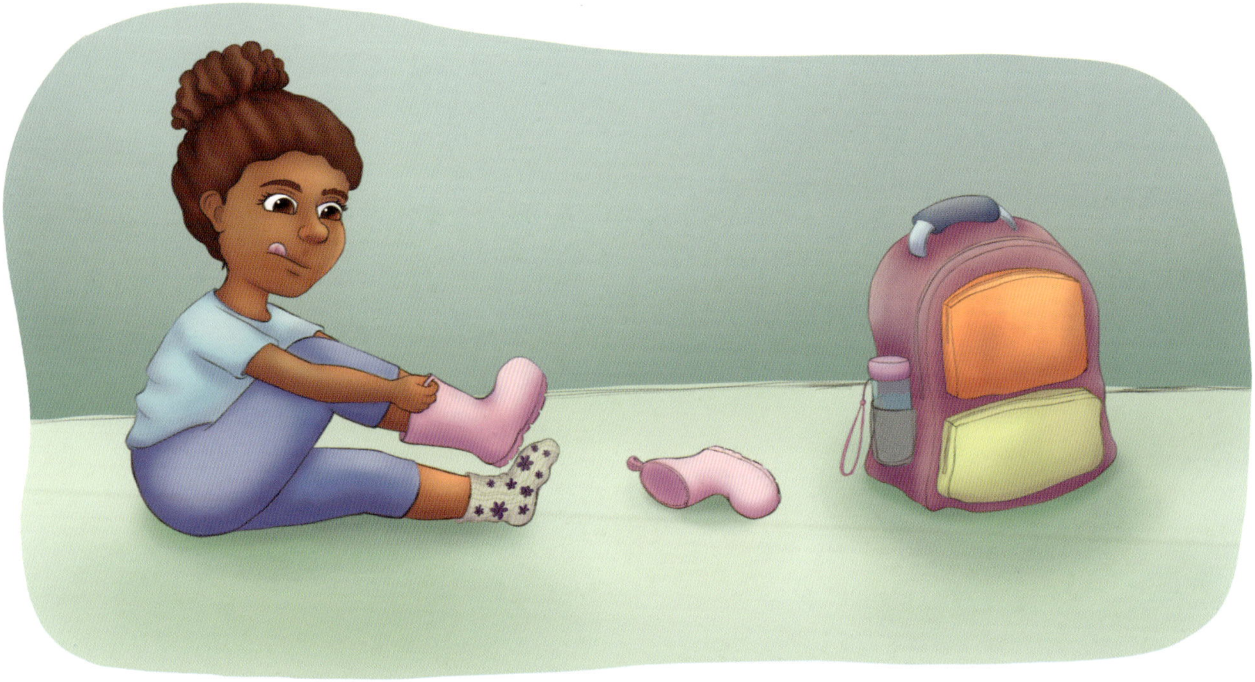

Library of Congress Number 2020950879

ISBN 978-1-7356391-0-9

Printed in China

First Edition 10 9 8 7 6 5 4 3 2 1

Saturdays with Daddy

Katrina Johnson
and Zaria Johnson

Illustrated by
Rhododendron Art

Sunshine Books
Richmond

Hi! Today my mom is taking me to the farm to visit my dad. He says that he has a **surprise** for me.

We're at the **farm**.

My dad grows all sorts of things at the farm. He grows strawberries, blueberries, raspberries, kale, tomatoes, garlic, and other yummy fruits and vegetables.

Look, here is my **surprise!**
My dad is giving me a garden of my own.

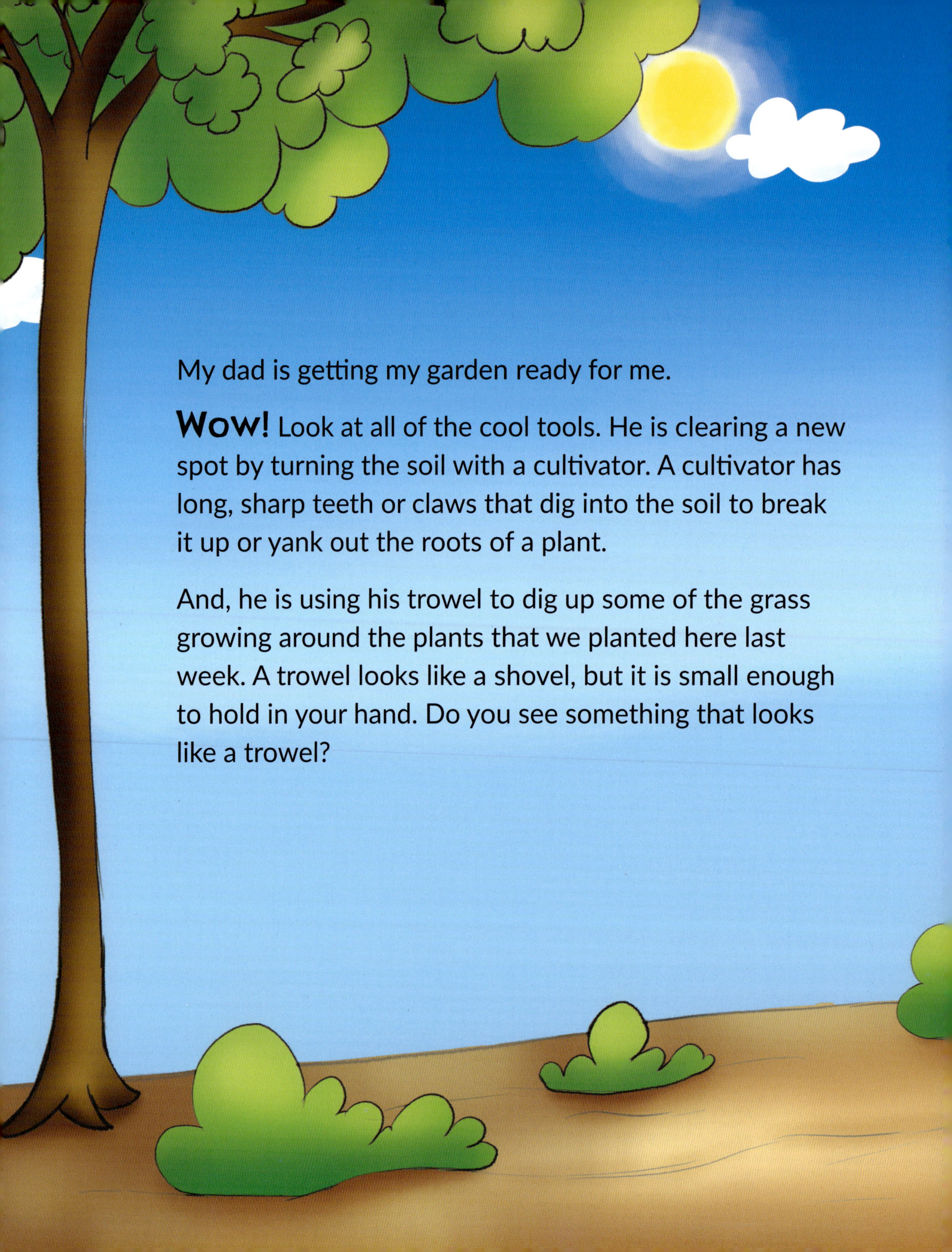

My dad is getting my garden ready for me.

Wow! Look at all of the cool tools. He is clearing a new spot by turning the soil with a cultivator. A cultivator has long, sharp teeth or claws that dig into the soil to break it up or yank out the roots of a plant.

And, he is using his trowel to dig up some of the grass growing around the plants that we planted here last week. A trowel looks like a shovel, but it is small enough to hold in your hand. Do you see something that looks like a trowel?

Now, he wants to see what tools I brought with me.

Let's see what I have in my backpack. I have a bottle of water, a notebook, a bucket, a blanket, a watering can, a hat, trowel, sunglasses, hand wipes, and sunscreen.

My dad plops my hat on my head and tells me to grab my notebook and to get ready for my lesson.

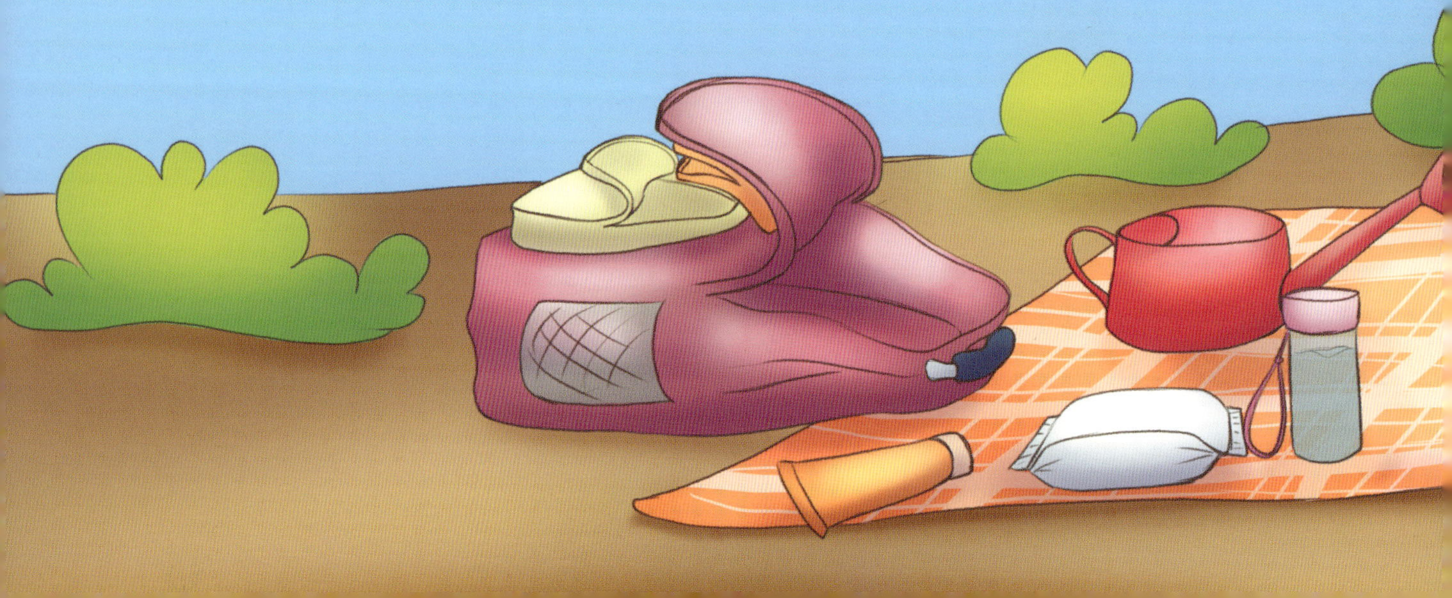

The next thing we do is talk about **O.W.W.**,
and my dad asks me if I remember what it means.

The "**O**" is for **observations**. Making observations
is the first thing that I have to do to make sure
I take good care of my garden.
The first "**W**" is for **weed**. I have to make sure that
I pull out any weeds that I see when I am observing.
And, the last "**W**" is for **water**. I have to see
if my plants look thirsty and make sure I check
the soil to see if it needs some water.

O.W.W.

It's time to observe.

Hmm, what do I see?

Do I have any plants coming up through the soil?

Do my plants look healthy?

Are there any weeds?

Does the soil look dry?

Now, let me see. Have any animals been by to play and nibble on the plants in the garden?

My dad and I grow all of our fruits and vegetables without chemicals. He calls it **permaculture**. So, I pay close attention to see if there are any plants that I don't want in my garden, we call those weeds, or any animals or bugs that I don't want, we call those **pests**.

Did you know that some insects are helpers? Like bees and butterflies.

Daddy said it is time for me to get out my trowel. Let's weed.

As we pull up the grass that is trying to grow where I planted arugula and swiss chard — boy, that's hard to say. Daddy tells me that I may have just enough space to plant two more things. So, I decided to take a break and grabbed some seeds from his box. I picked watermelon seeds and spinach seeds.

My dad said those were good choices. He called them **superfoods**. He said they are yummy and help you stay healthy.

I take my trowel and make a little hole. Then I drop three seeds in the hole and cover it with soil. All done.

Oh, let me add a little marker with the plant names to help me find them while I wait for my seeds to grow into a plant and break through the soil.

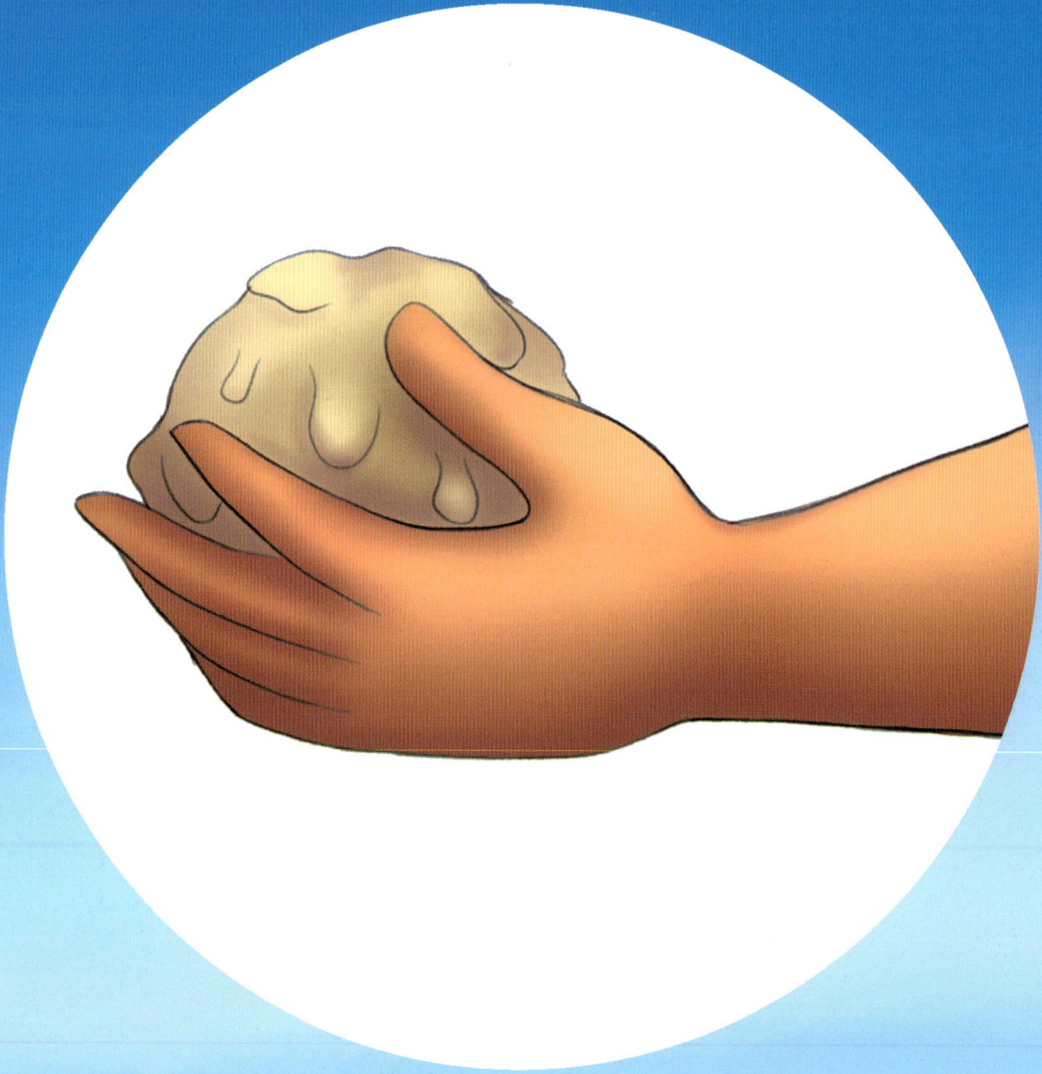

Now, I have to check to see if we need to give the plants some water. First, I take a look at the soil. It doesn't look dry. But I want to be sure, so I take my trowel and make a little hole in the soil, near the plants, and stick my finger in it. It feels wet. Then I grab a little dirt from the trowel and try to make it into a ball. It's just like playing with clay or dough in art class.

Look, I made a ball! It looks like I don't need my watering can today.

I OBSERVED,

I WEEDED, and

I WATERED my plants.

I am all done for the day.
Now I can hunt for earthworms.

Found one! Earthworms are little helpers
in my garden. They help keep the soil healthy.

Did you know that worms are not insects?
Both worms and insects are animals.

I think I hear my mom calling me.

It must be time to pick some berries to take to grandma.

Let me go clean my hands and grab my bucket.

Ooo, the strawberries are ready for picking.
They are so yummy.

It’s time to say goodbye to daddy
and head off to my grandparents’ house.

I can’t wait to find out what we are going to make.

I rinsed the strawberries.

Grammy said to only rinse the strawberries that we are using and to put the dry ones in the refrigerator.

We are making strawberry shortcake.
Can you find grandma's recipe?

STRAWBERRY SHORTCAKE

BERRIES
4 cups **strawberries**
⅓ cup **granulated sugar**

WHIPPED CREAM
2 ¼ cups **heavy whipping cream**
8 ounces **cream cheese**, softened
1/2 cup **powdered sugar**

SHORTCAKE
3 cups flour
1 ¼ cups **granulated sugar**
1 tablespoon **baking powder**
½ teaspoon **baking soda**
½ teaspoon **salt**
2 ½ sticks **unsalted butter**, softened
4 large **eggs**
1 cup **heavy whipping cream**
1 teaspoon **vanilla extract**

DIRECTIONS

STRAWBERRIES

Rinse the strawberries and remove the hulls. Slice the strawberries and place them in a large bowl. Combine strawberries and sugar together in bowl, toss to coat.

SHORTCAKE

1. Preheat oven to 350°F. Grease three 9-inch round cake pans.

2. In a medium bowl, sift together the flour, baking powder, baking soda and salt. Set aside.

3. In a measuring cup or bowl, mix the heaving whipping cream and vanilla extract. Set aside.

4. In a large mixing bowl and using a hand mixer, cream together the softened butter and granulated sugar for about 4-5 minutes until creamy.

5. Add the eggs one at a time lightly beating after each one is added.

6. Add the sifted dry ingredients alternately with the heavy whipping cream and vanilla extract. Beat on medium speed until combined, then increase the speed of the mixer and beat for 1-2 minutes.

7. Divide the batter evenly between the cake pans.
Tip: Use an icing knife to make distributing and smoothing the thick batter easier.

8. Bake for 20-25 minutes or until a toothpick inserted in the center comes back clean. Remove cakes from the oven and let them cool completely on a wire rack.
Tip: Use a long-serrated knife to trim and level the top of each layer.

WHIPPED CREAM

In a large mixing bowl beat the cream cheese until smooth. Add the powdered sugar and beat until blended. With the mixer on low, slowly add the whipping cream mixing until incorporated. Turn the mixer to high and beat until creamy but stiff peaks form.

ASSEMBLY

Center one cake on a cake stand. Top with 1/3 whipped cream and sliced strawberries. Repeat the process with the second layer. For final layer, top with whipped cream and garnish with the remaining berries.

Mommy and I are back home now.

Daddy says that he is **proud** of me and that I did a great job taking care of my garden today.

Thanks
for spending
the day
with me!

Ready for More Fun!

Find and circle all of the words in the list below.

v	g	a	r	d	e	n	b	e	j
o	y	t	j	s	o	i	l	g	m
w	b	r	z	l	u	a	k	f	r
a	c	e	h	q	a	s	e	e	d
t	v	e	g	e	t	a	b	l	e
e	j	k	f	i	s	h	y	d	z
r	o	g	x	r	u	c	v	b	a
d	j	o	u	r	n	a	l	e	r
c	f	l	o	w	e	r	z	e	i
f	r	u	i	t	u	s	i	h	a

vegetable	journal	flower	water
fruit	garden	seed	bee
soil	zaria	tree	sun

Help Zaria find the right path to get to her garden.